A little chicken was playing on the grass by the bush. He saw a robin fly down from the sky and land in the bush.

"I am going to fly, just like the robin," said the little chicken to himself. "I will flap my wings and fly in the sky."

He ran along the grass ... flap ... flap ... flap. He jumped up ... fly ... fly ... fly ... flop ... flop ... PLOP. He fell on the grass.

He began to cry. The robin came to see him. "I can't fly," he said to the robin. "Why? ... Why can't I fly?"

"Don't cry," said the robin. "I will teach you to fly. Just flap your wings like me, and take off into the sky."

The robin flapped his wings and took off into the sky. Whoosh! He was flying over the bushes and trees.

The chicken flapped his wings and jumped up ... but ... flop ... PLOP! He was lying on the grass.

The chicken began to cry again. "Why can't I fly?" he said to the robin. "I try and try, but I can't fly."

"I think your wings are too little to fly," said the robin, "but they will grow. Then you can try to fly again."

So the little chicken went to look for the hen. She would look after him until his wings were bigger. Then he would try to fly again.

"y"

by

fly

cry

lying

flying

sky

why

my

try

High Frequency Words

a was on the he and in I
am going to like said up my
are can went look for she see
me they you playing

little saw down from just ran
can't why don't will by take
off his took but our too again
would so after him were then
came jumped